Charles Perry's INTRODUCTION to the DRUM SET

INSTRUCTIONS for

BASS DRUM
right foot

HI HAT
left foot
right hand

SNARE DRUM
left hand

BRUSH BEATS

ELEMENTARY DRUM BREAKS

FOREWORD

Since it is essential to the popular phase of drumming (Jazz-Show-Dance), the "Drum Set" has become an integral part of the contemporary drum instructors method of teaching. Hence, the purpose of this book is a functional one, as it is designed to develop "Drum Set Technique" and the corresponding elements of jazz (Jazz form) drumming.

The material contained herein is intended to supplement, rather than to replace, the three mainstays of drumming: Rudiments, Reading, and Technique.

CHARLIE PERRY

During the World War II, Charles Perry was with the Official United States Coast Guard Band, in Washington, D.C. He played in the Concert Band, and was First Drummer in the Swing Band, radio and Show Band.

He has worked with such name bands as Benny Goodman, Stan Kenton, Buddy Morrow, Skitch Henderson, Alvino Rey and Woody Herman.

In the small modern jazz group, he has played with Stan Getz, Kai Winding, Al Haig and Bud Powell. This latter groups, Powells had Gene Ramey on Bass, Wardell Gray and Sonny Stitt on tenors and Bud Powell on Piano.

He has recorded for Capitol, Mercury, RCA Victor and Columbia and has played for such artists on these records as Patti Page, Kitty Kalen, Teddi King and many others. He has also made many jazz records with Stan Getz, Al Haig, Wardell Gray, Johnny LaPorta and other Jazz Stars.

He has studied with many teachers, among those Alfred Friese at the Manhattan School of Music, Billy Gladstone of Radio City Music Hall and Henry Adler.

TABLE OF CONTENTS

Set Routine No. 1

Brushes on Snare Drum

DIAGRAM 1

Right Brush
2
4

Right Brush
1
3

Left Brush
1 → 2
3 ←
→ 4

Left Hand Brush swishes from side to side.

Right Hand Brush plays first stroke on right side of snare drum.

Second stroke is played on left side of snare drum. (Right brush crosses over left brush.)

Third Stroke is played on right side of snare drum.

Fourth stroke is played on left side of snare drum. (Right brush crosses over left brush.)

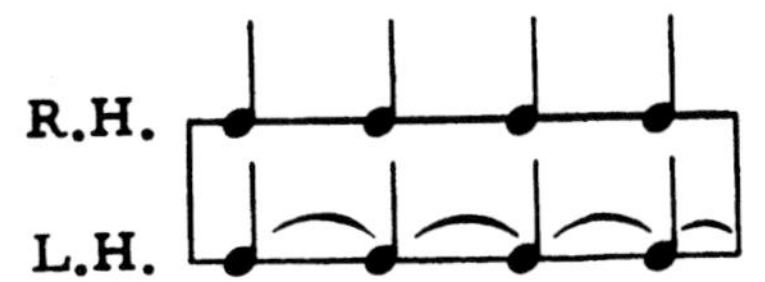

Cross as in Diagram 1

Swish as in Diagram 1

Set Routine No. 2

Bass Drum on 1 2 3 4
Hi Hat on 2 and 4

R.H. Taps

L.H. Swishes

B.D. Right Foot

Hi Hat Left Foot

Set Routine No. 3

Bass Drum on 1 and 3
Hi Hat on 2 and 4

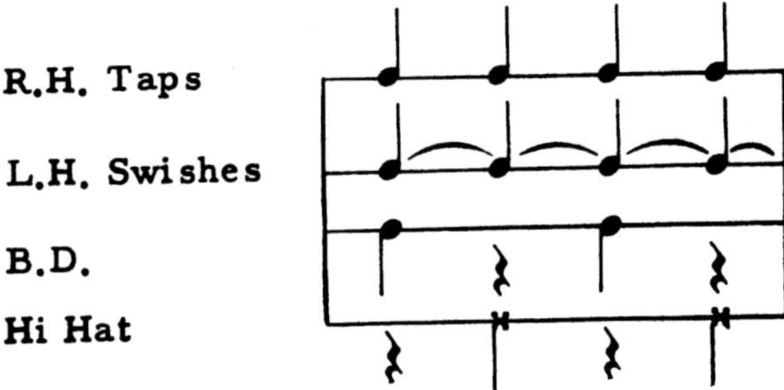

Set Routine No. 4

Brushes on Snare Drum

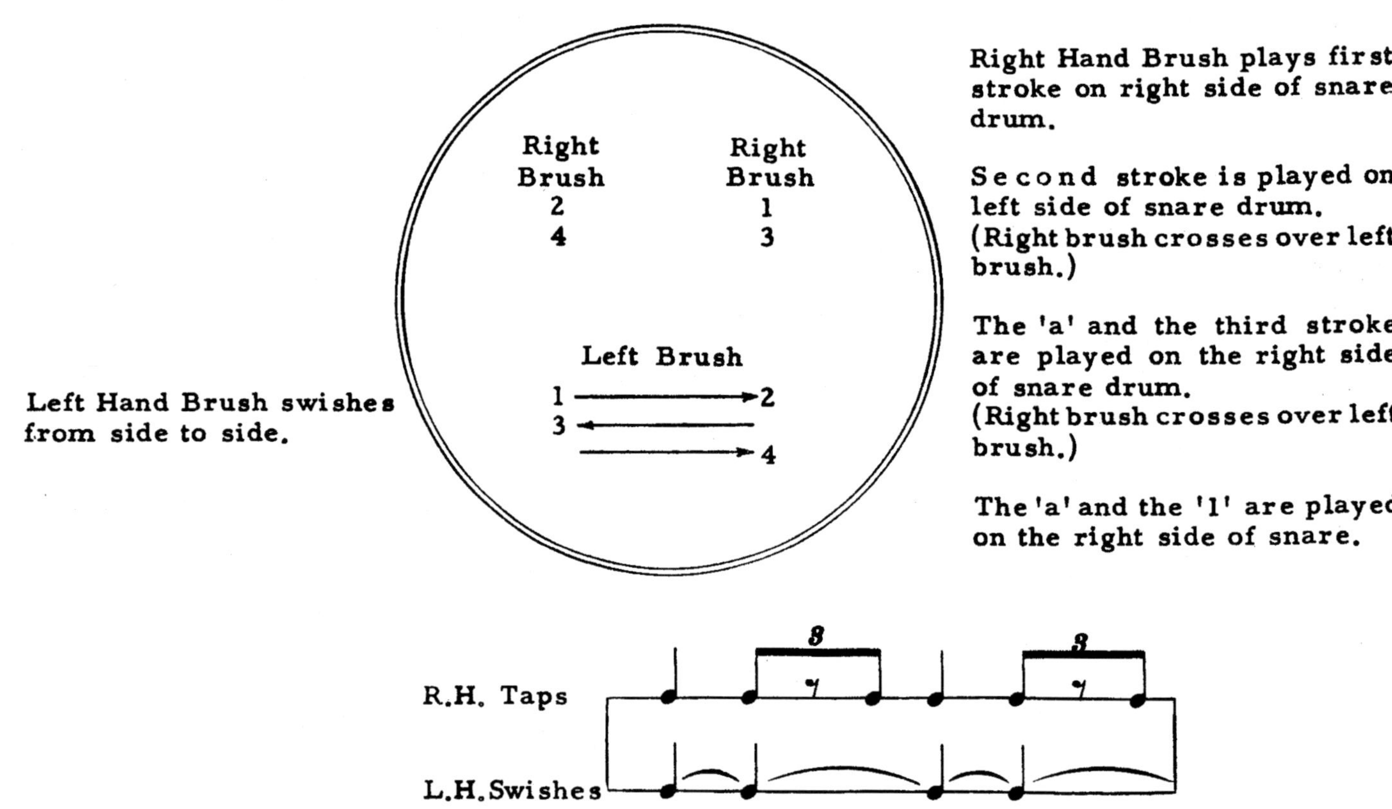

Right Hand Brush plays first stroke on right side of snare drum.

Second stroke is played on left side of snare drum. (Right brush crosses over left brush.)

The 'a' and the third stroke are played on the right side of snare drum. (Right brush crosses over left brush.)

The 'a' and the '1' are played on the right side of snare.

Set Routine No. 5

Bass Drum on 1 2 3 4
Hi Hat on 2 and 4

Set Routine No. 6

Bass Drum on 1 and 3
Hi Hat on 2 and 4

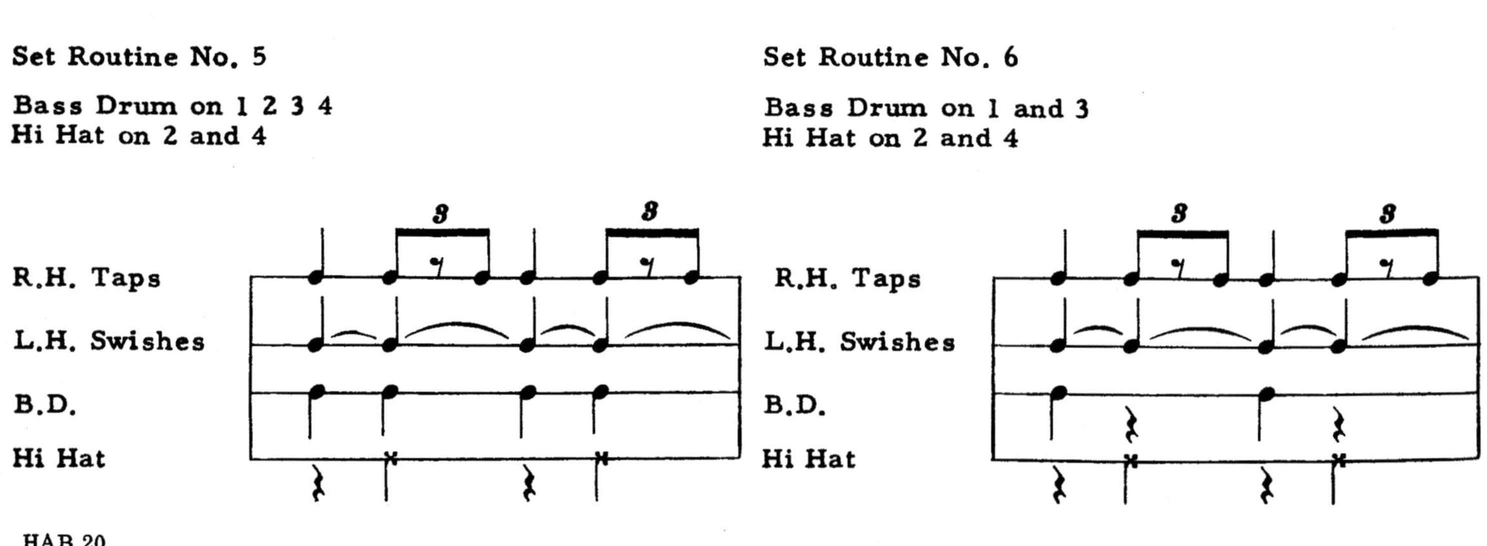

CYMBAL RHYTHMS (1)

This is the way "Cymbal Ride Rhythm" is normally written in drum music.

(A)

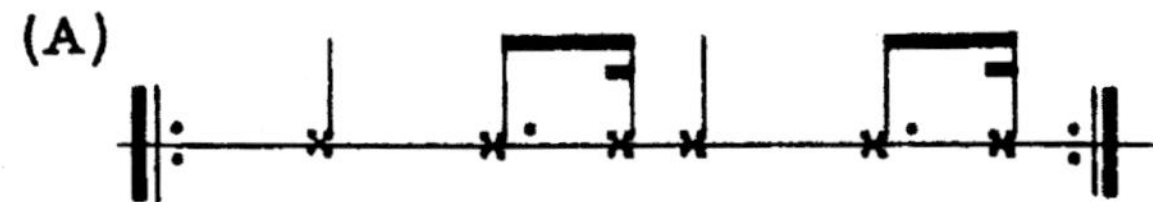

This is the way most drummers play the "Cymbal Ride Rhythm" since it gives a swinging, loose and relaxed feeling.

(B)

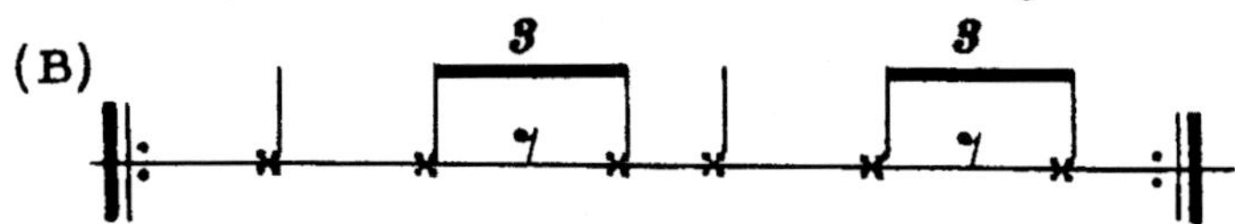

In the book, cymbal rhythms are written both ways, but student should play example B, excepting wherein noted.

RIGHT HAND AND BASS DRUM ROUTINES

(1) RH Cym / BD

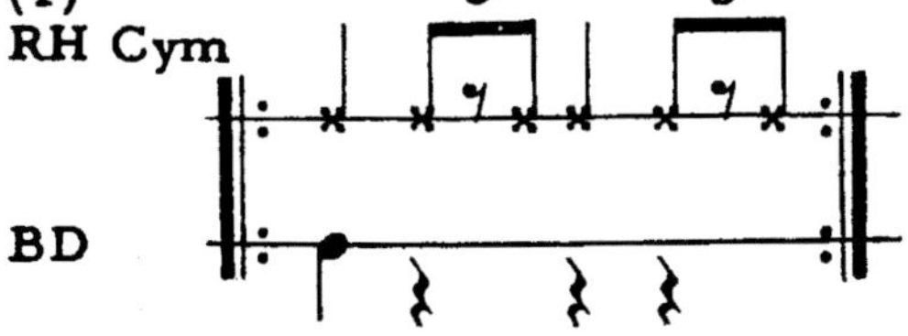

(2) RH Cym / BD

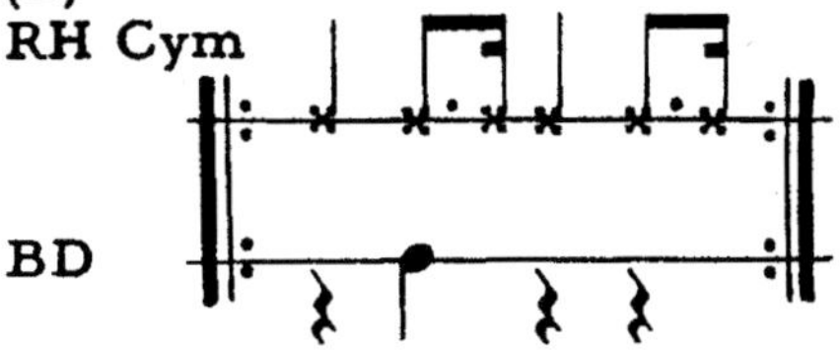

(3) RH Cym / BD

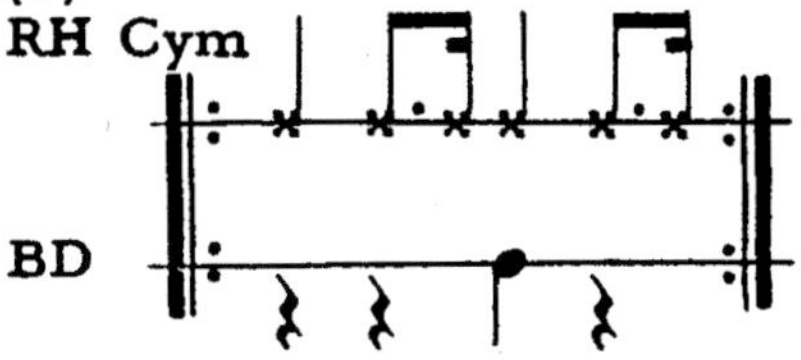

(4) RH Cym / BD

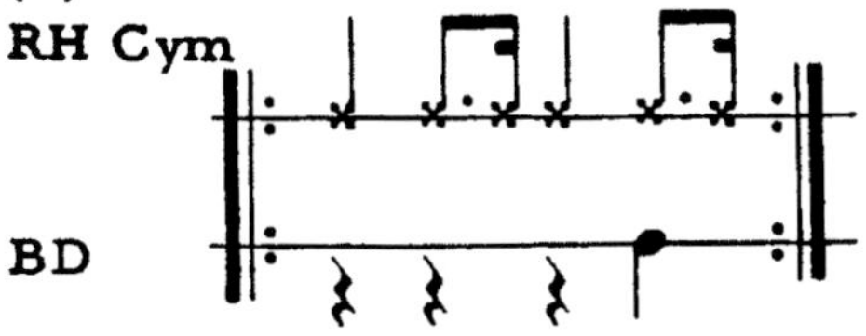

(5) RH Cym / BD

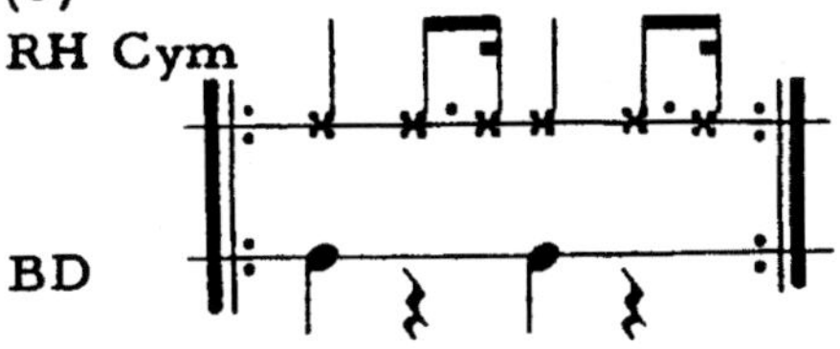

(6) RH Cym / BD

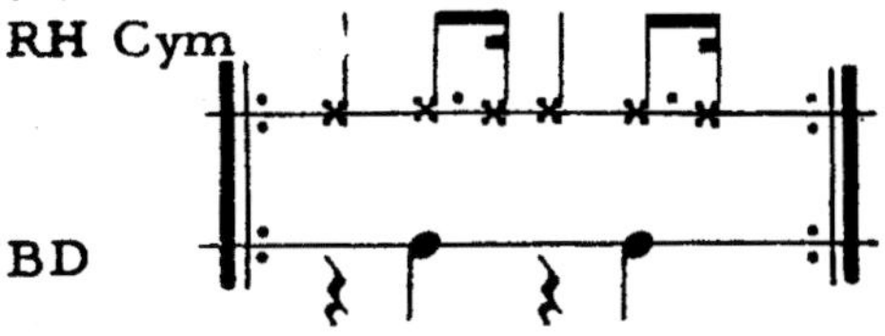

(7) RH Cym / BD

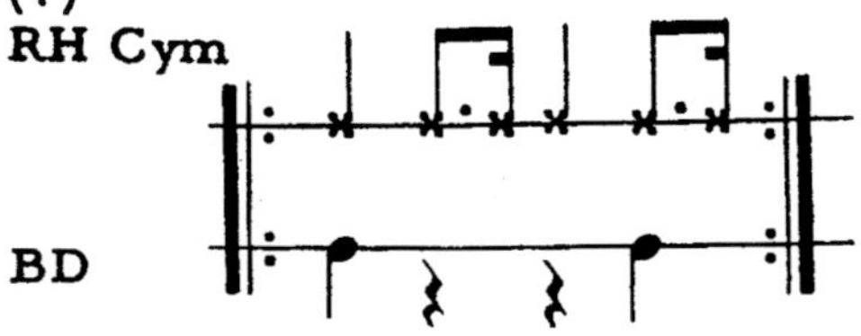

(8) RH Cym / BD

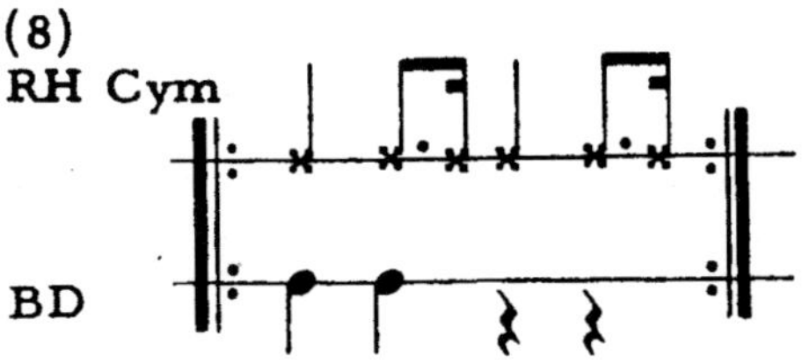

(9) RH Cym / BD

(10) RH Cym / BD

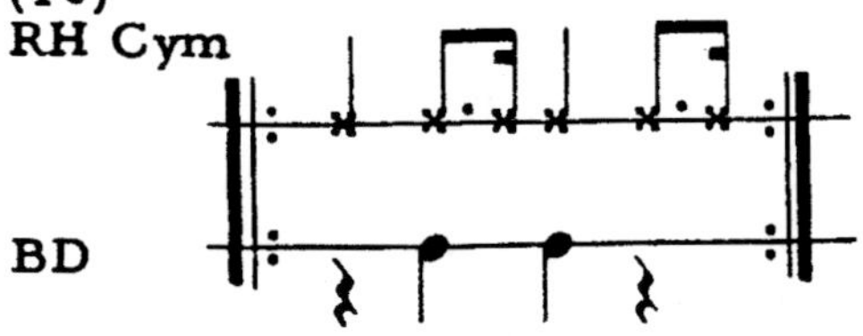

(11) RH Cym / BD

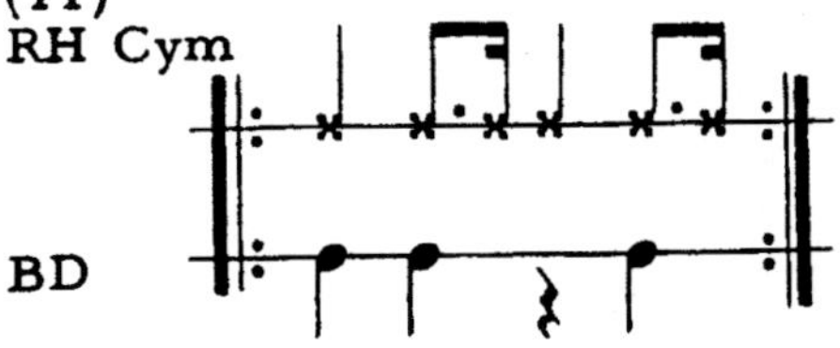

(12) RH Cym / BD

(13) RH Cym / BD

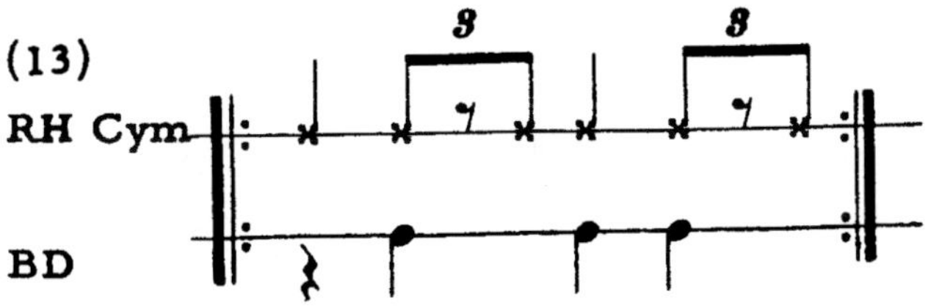

(14) RH Cym / BD

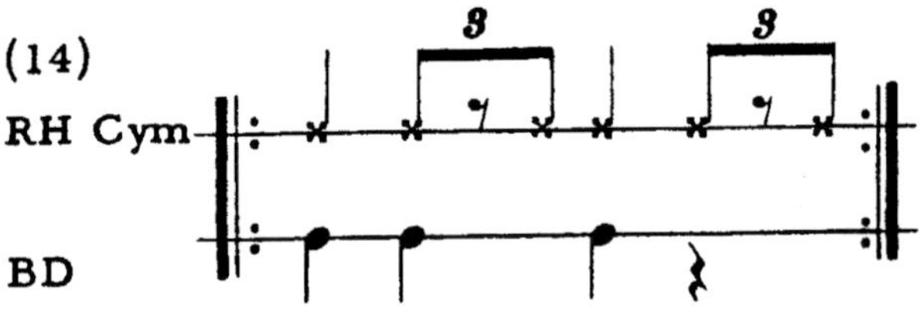

RIGHT HAND, BASS DRUM & HI HAT ROUTINES

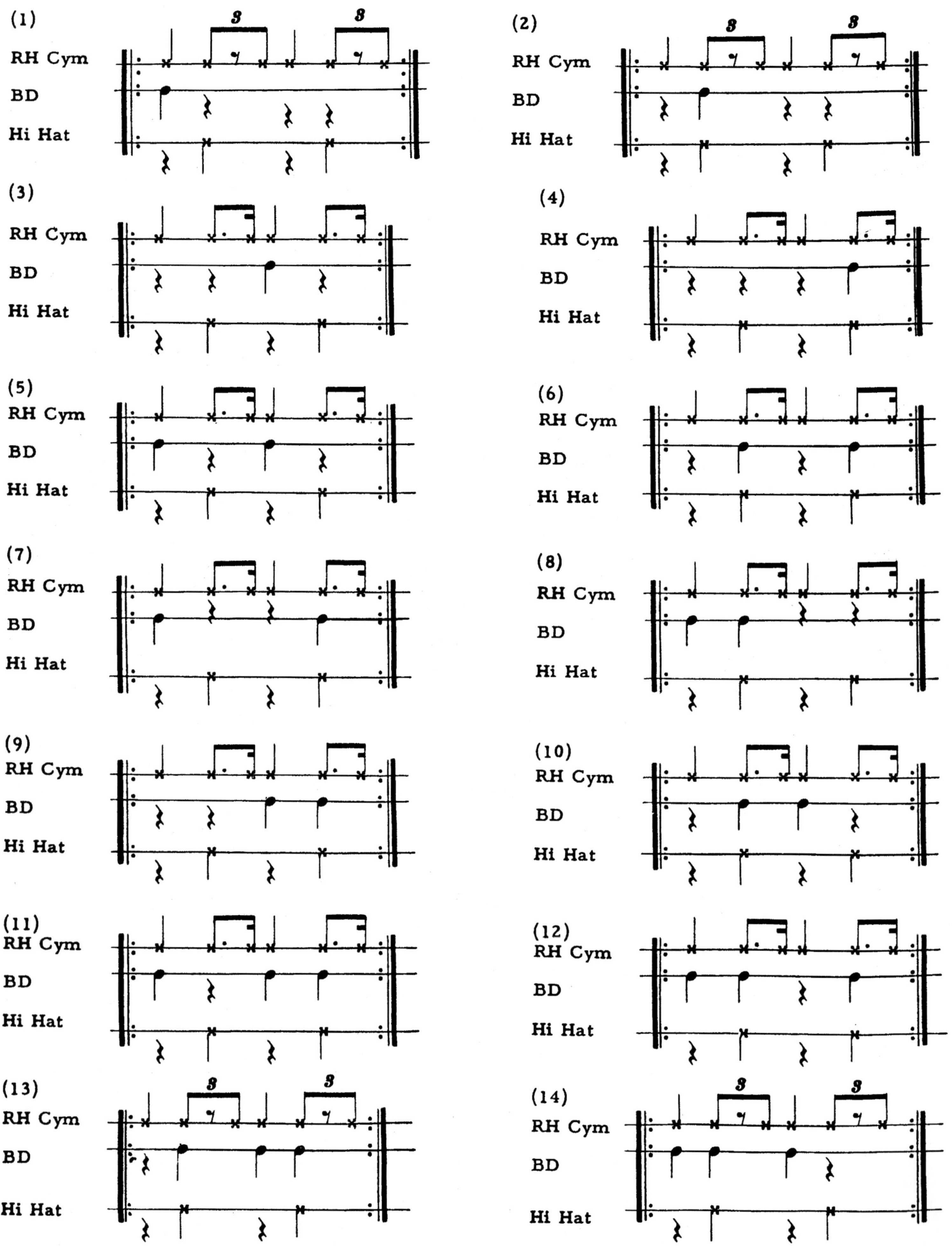

BASS DRUM ACCENTS

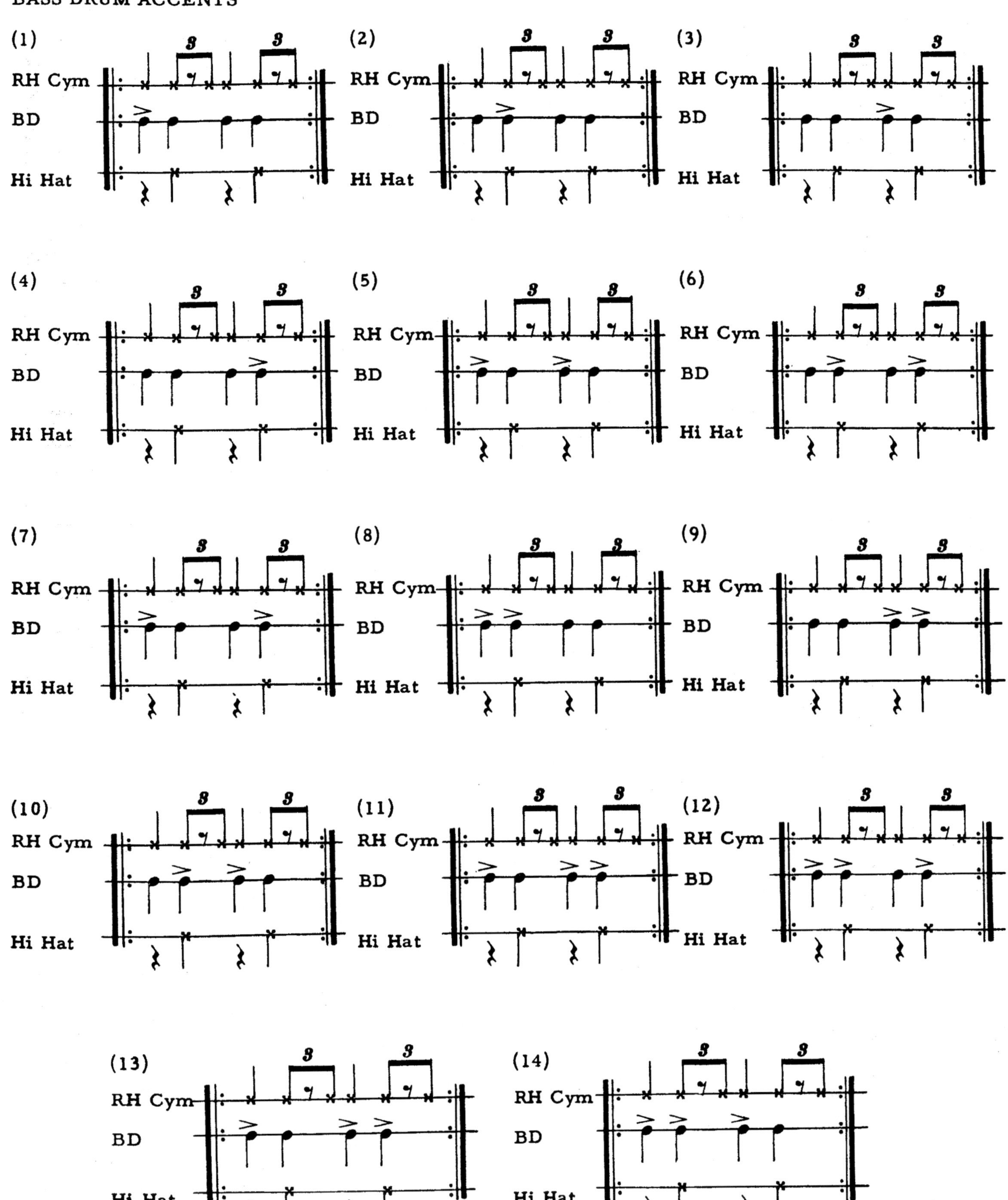

RIGHT HAND, LEFT HAND, BASS DRUM & HI HAT ROUTINES

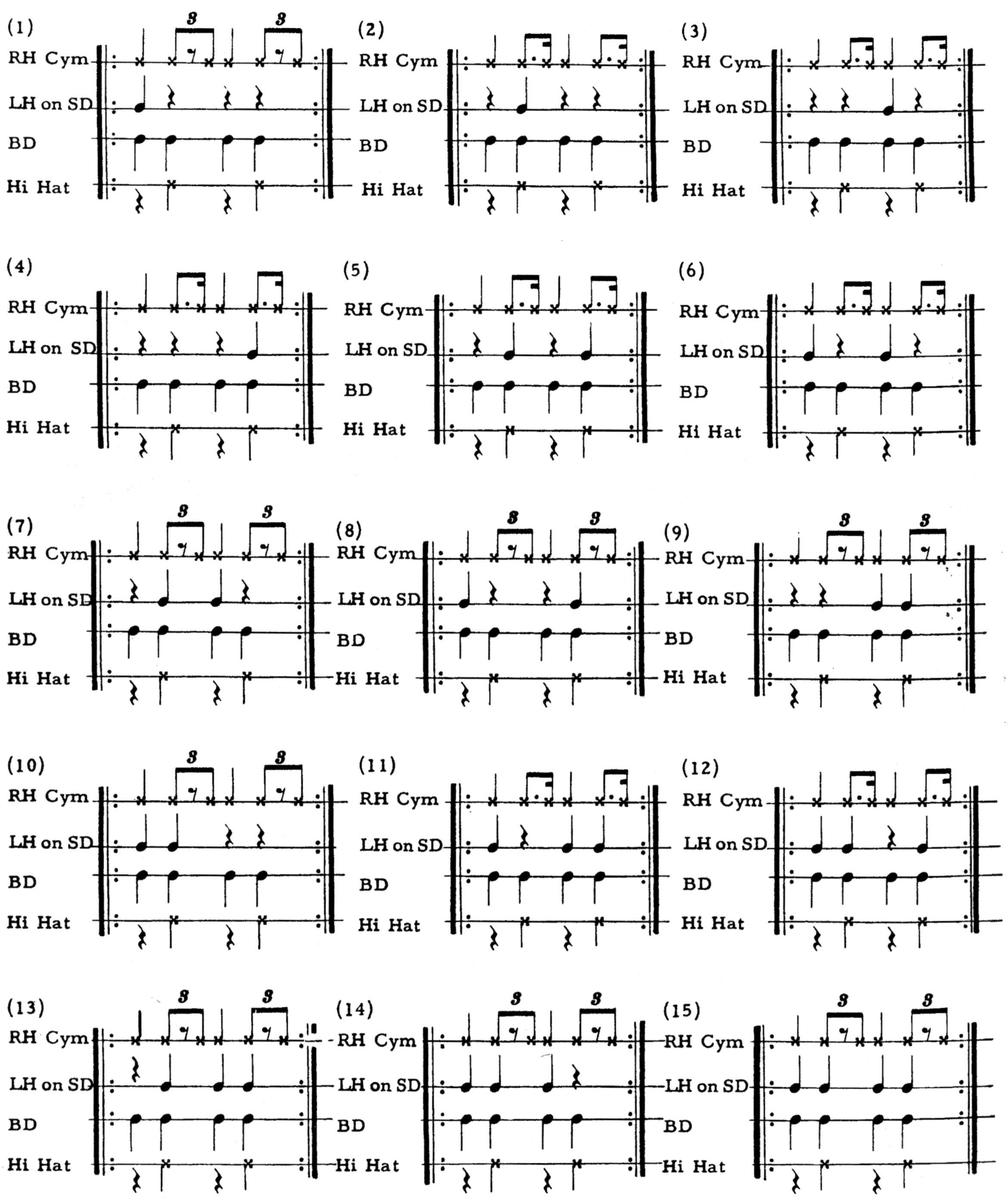

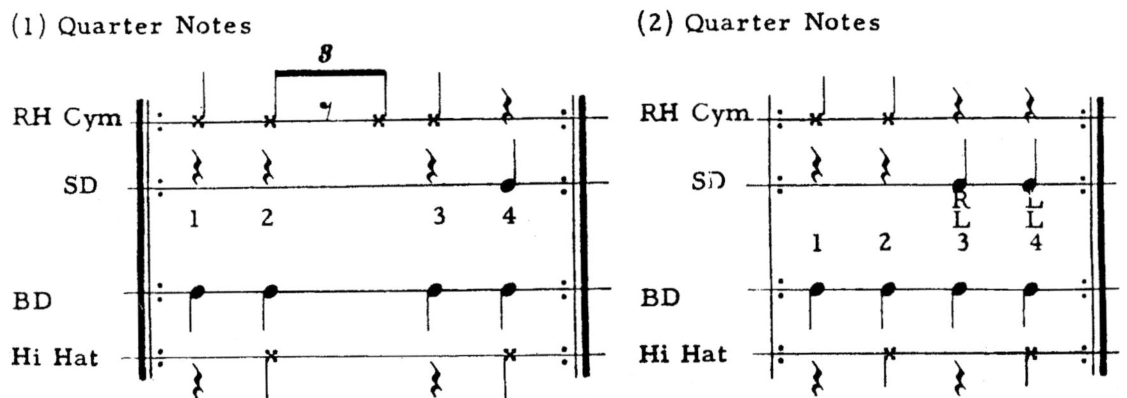

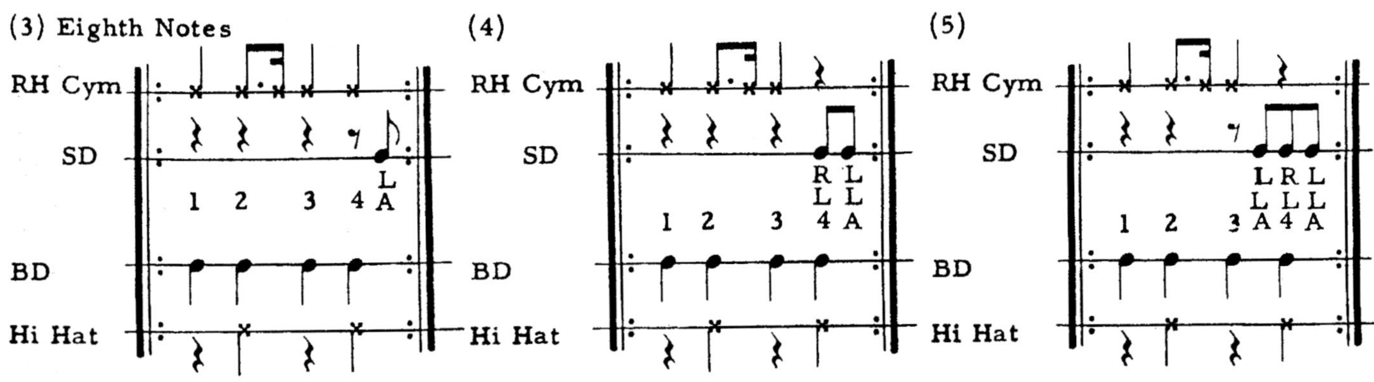

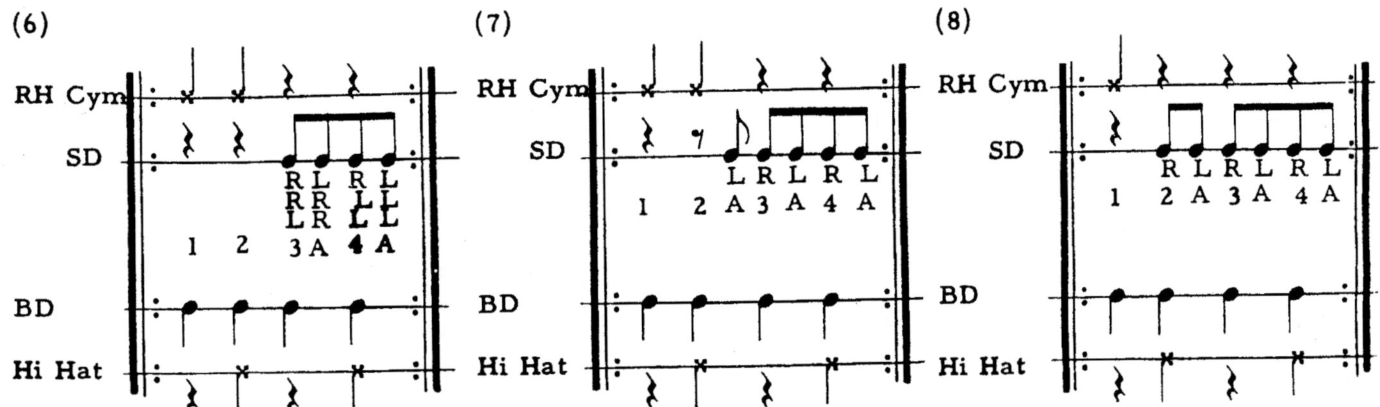

Can be played as five stroke ruff.
Can be played as five stroke roll.
Can be played as single paradiddle.

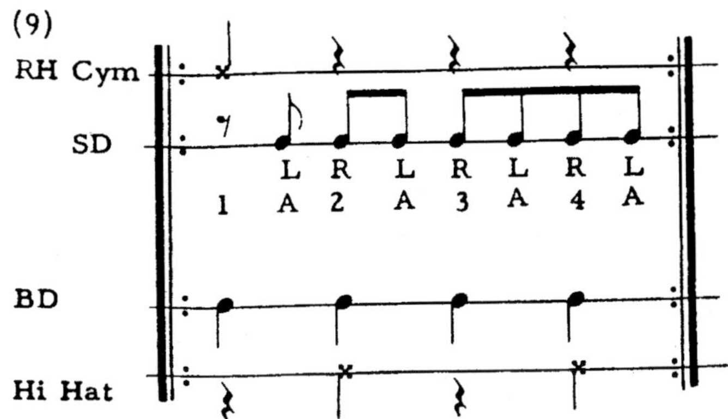

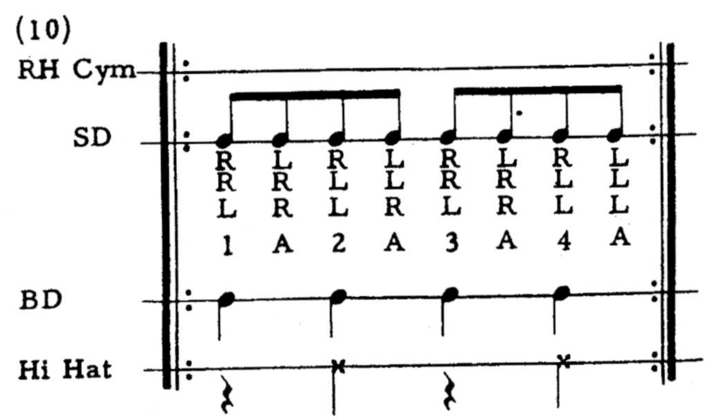

One measure fill-in, then return to ride rhythm.
(1) Play as single strokes
(2) Play as nine stroke roll
(3) Play as triple paradiddle

FILL-INS (Cont'd)

(11) Sixteenth Notes

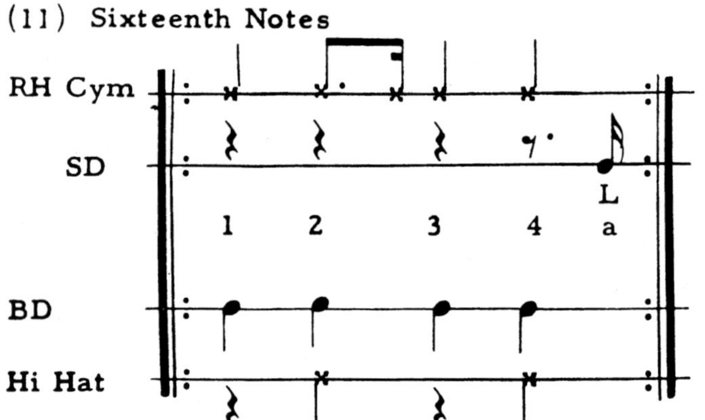

(12)

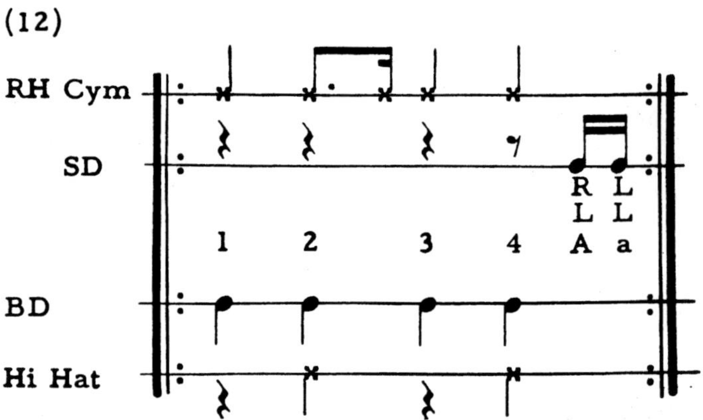

(13)

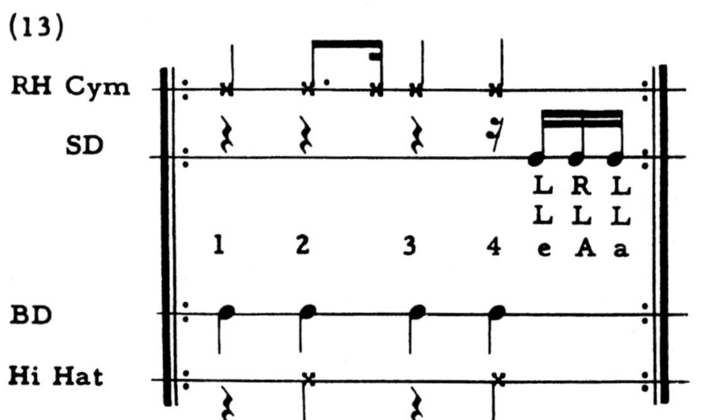

(14)

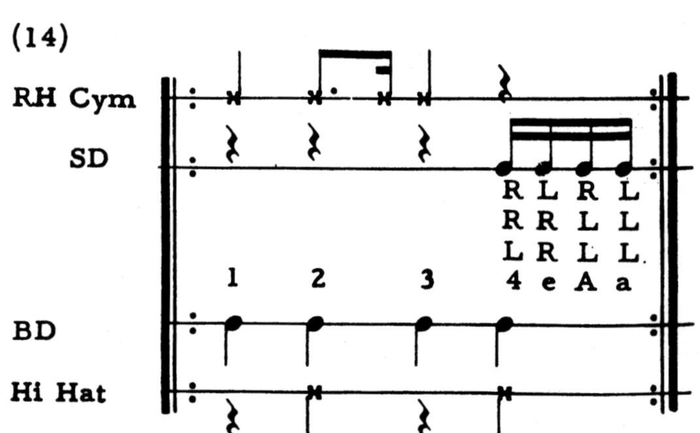

1. Play as Five Stroke Ruff
2. Play as Five Stroke Roll
3. Play as Single Paradiddle

(15)

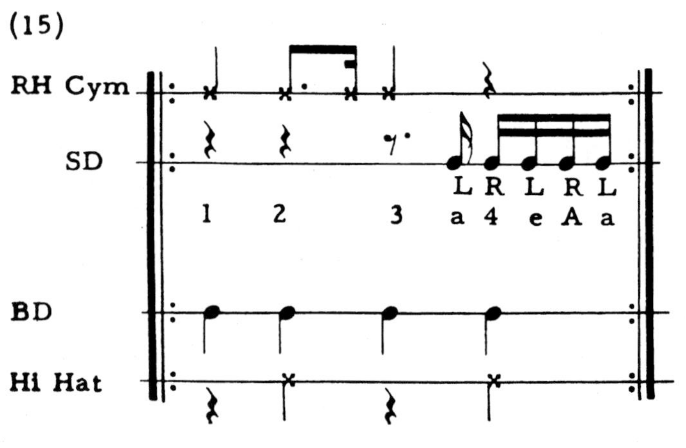

(16)

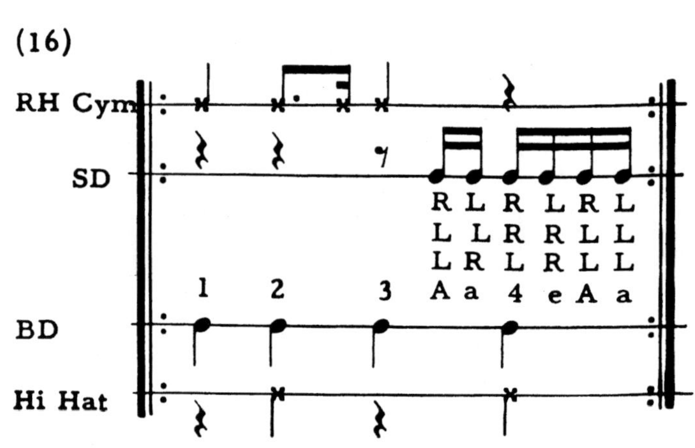

FILL-INS (Cont'd)

(17)

(18)

1. Play as Single Strokes
2. Play as Nine Stroke Roll
3. Play as Triple Paradiddle

(19)

(20)

(21) (22)

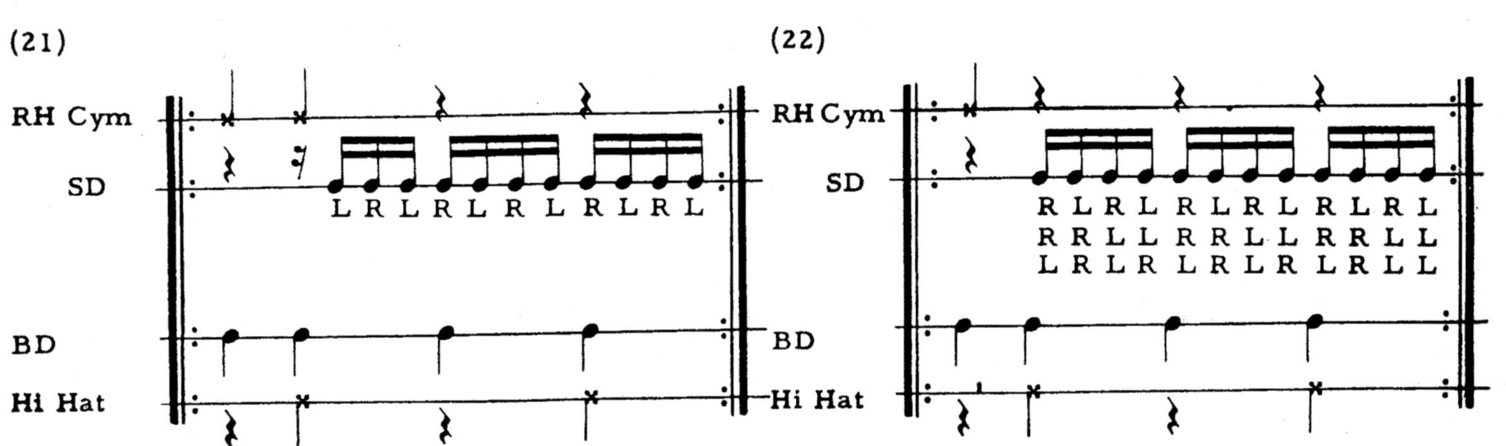

FILL-INS (Cont'd)

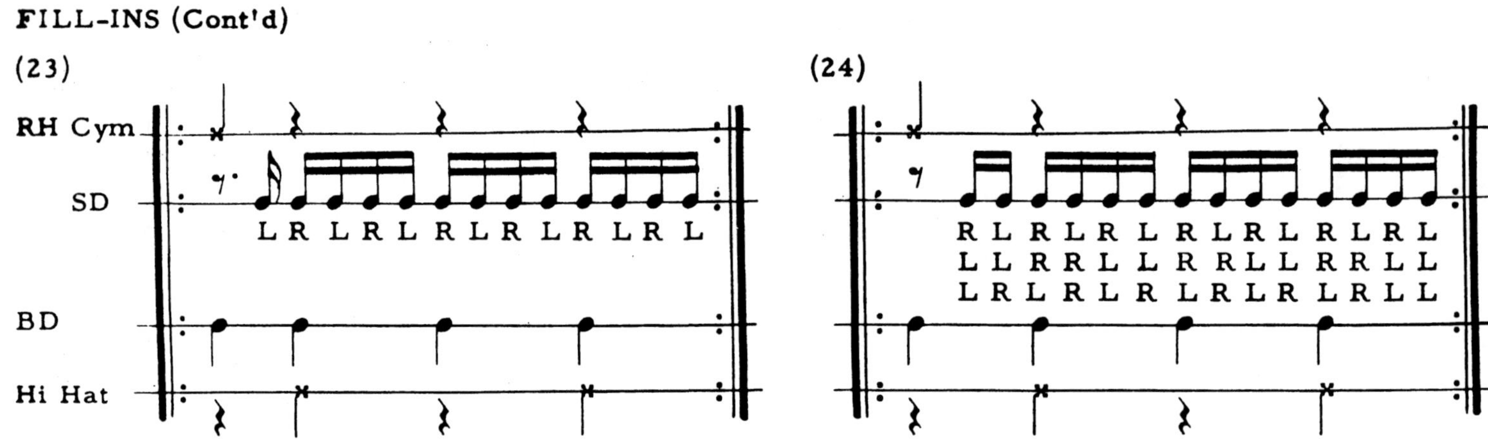

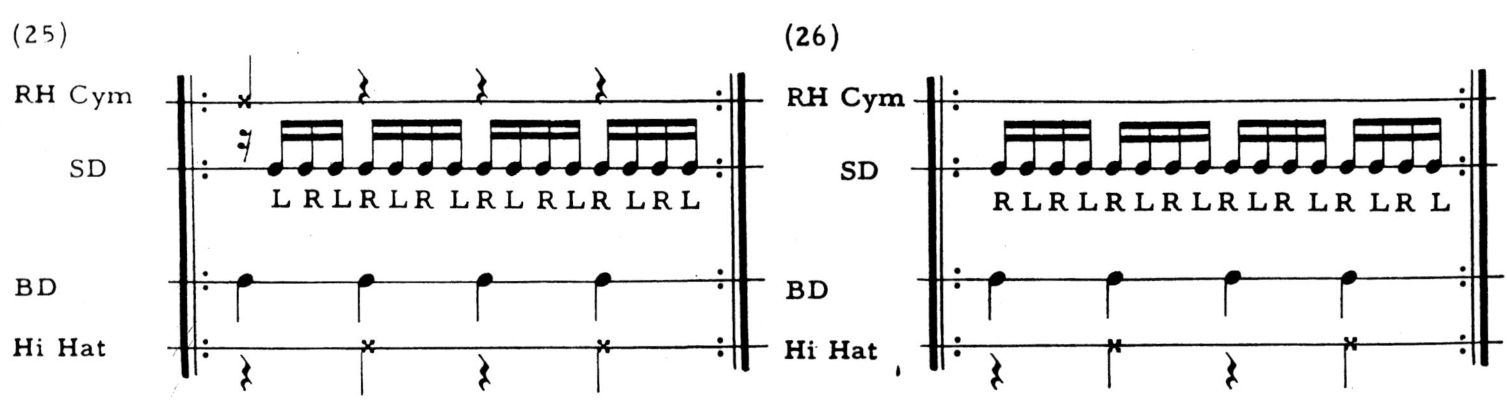

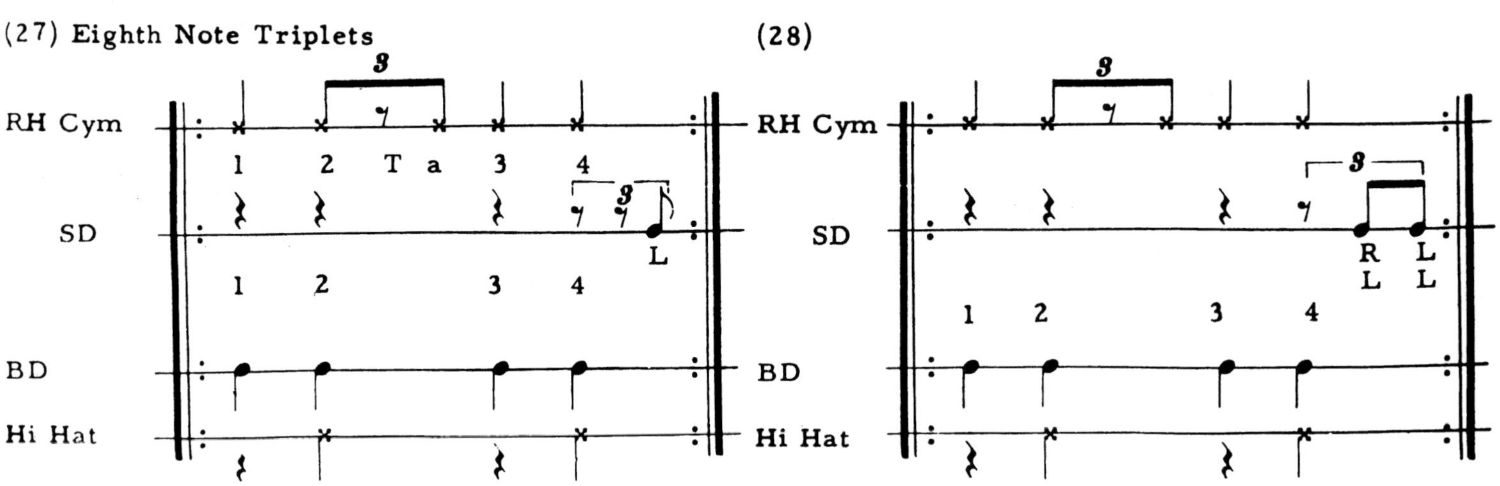

FILL-INS (Cont'd)

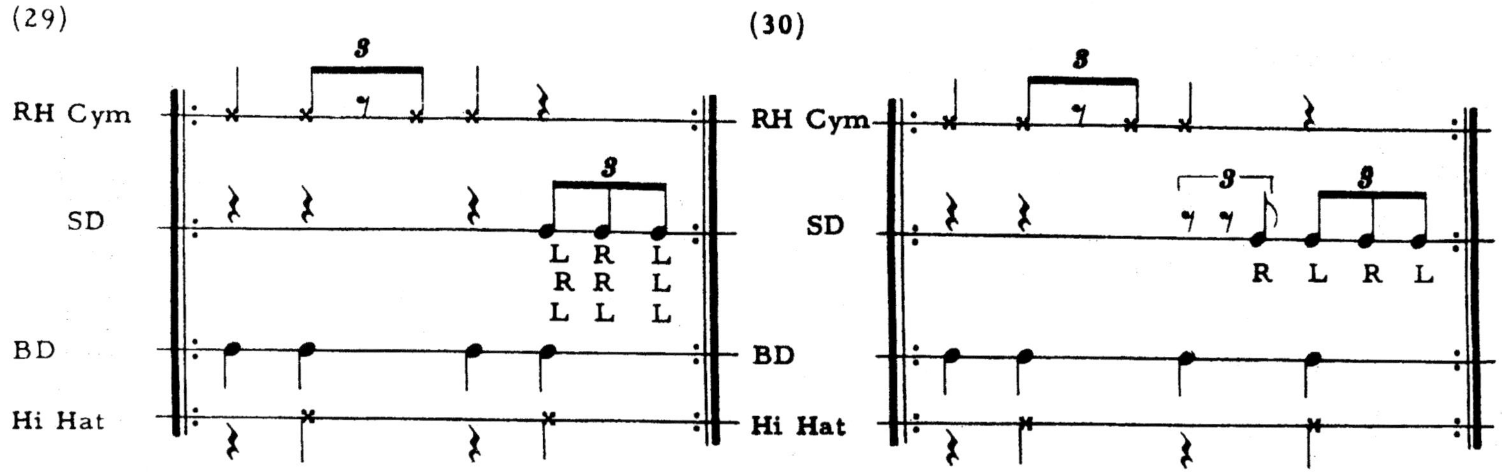

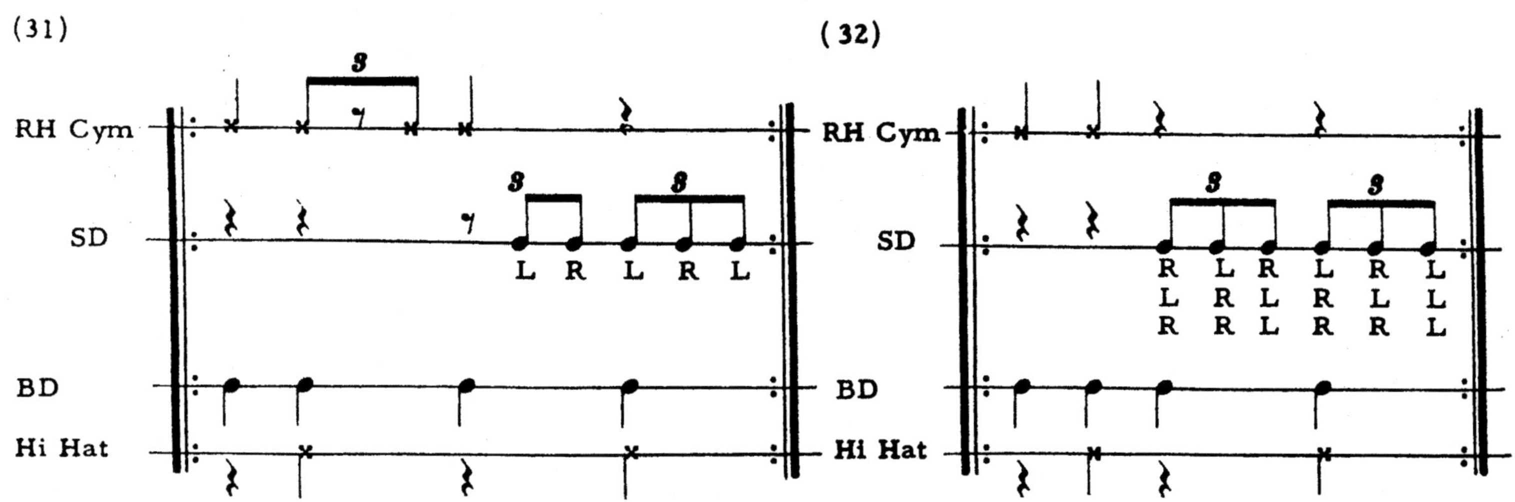

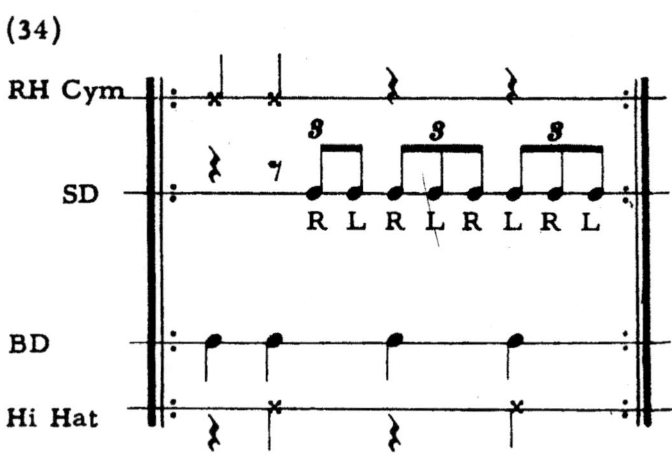

FILL-INS (Cont'd)

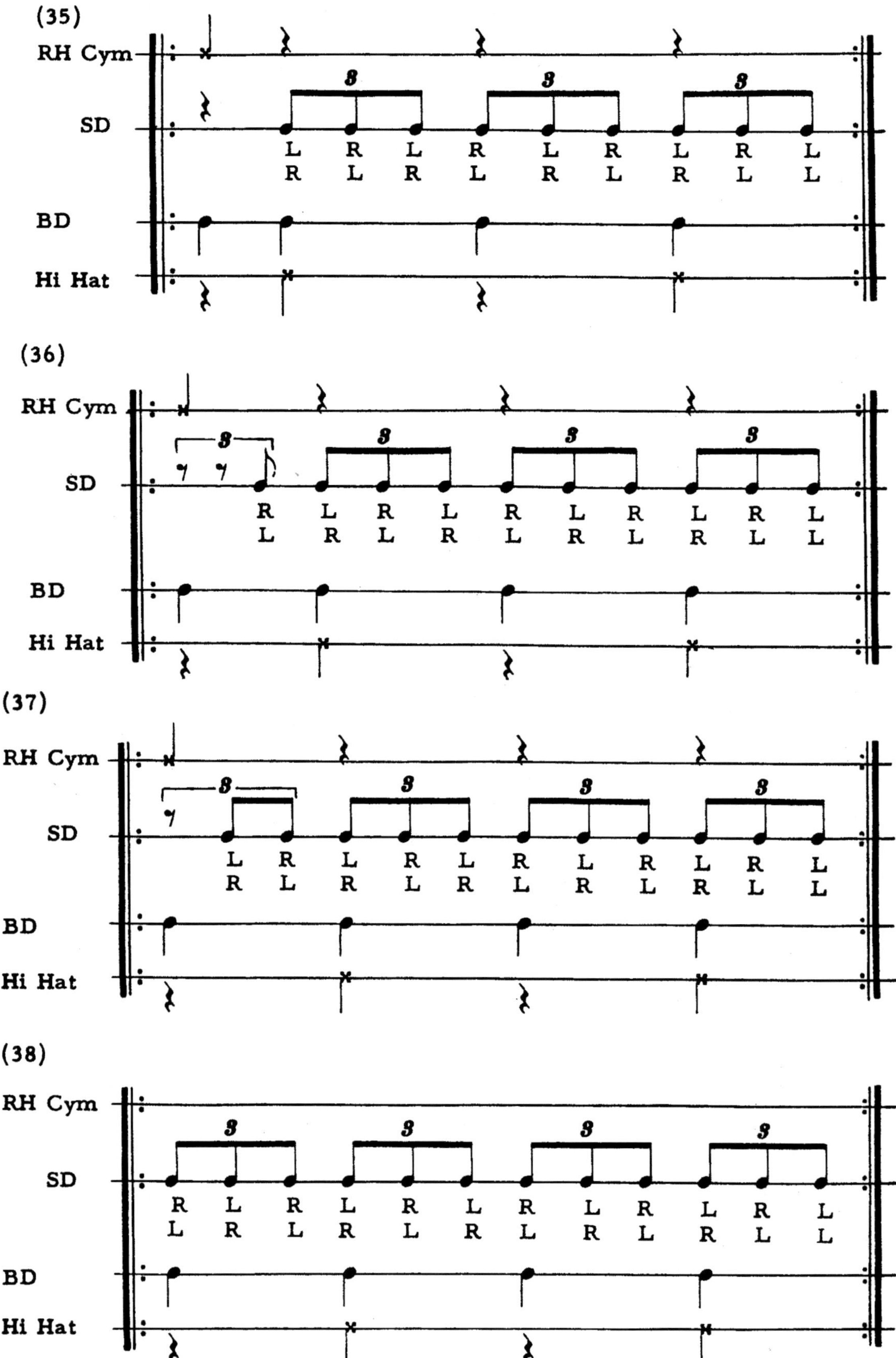

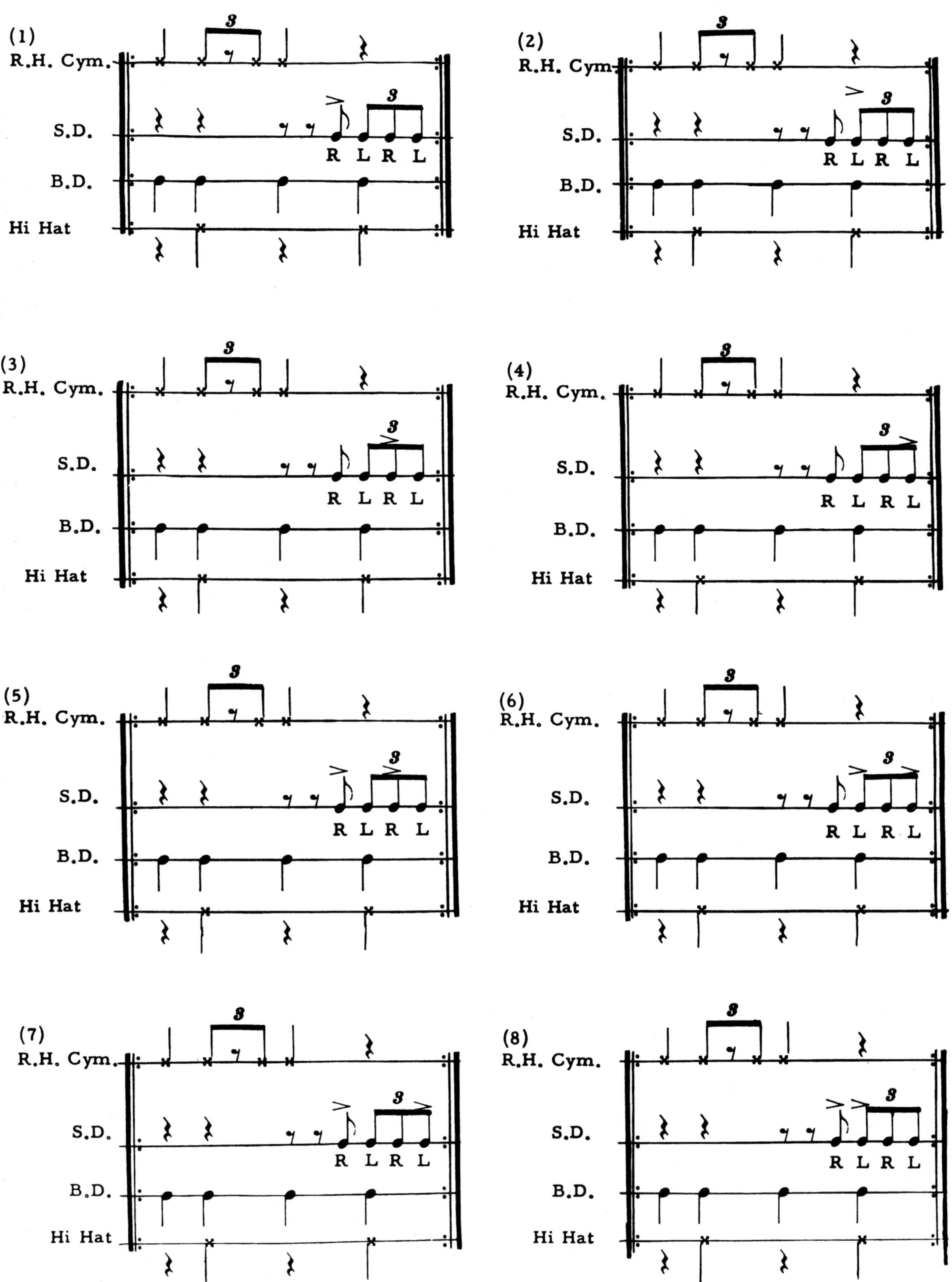
(1)
R.H. Cym.
S.D.
R L R L
B.D.
Hi Hat
(2)
R.H. Cym.
S.D.
R L R L
B.D.
Hi Hat
(3)
R.H. Cym.
S.D.
R L R L
B.D.
Hi Hat
(4)
R.H. Cym.
S.D.
R L R L
B.D.
Hi Hat
(5)
R.H. Cym.
S.D.
R L R L
B.D.
Hi Hat
(6)
R.H. Cym.
S.D.
R L R L
B.D.
Hi Hat
(7)
R.H. Cym.
S.D.
R L R L
B.D.
Hi Hat
(8)
R.H. Cym.
S.D.
R L R L
B.D.
Hi Hat

ACCENTED VARIATIONS OF SIXTEENTH NOTES - ROUTINE NO. 14

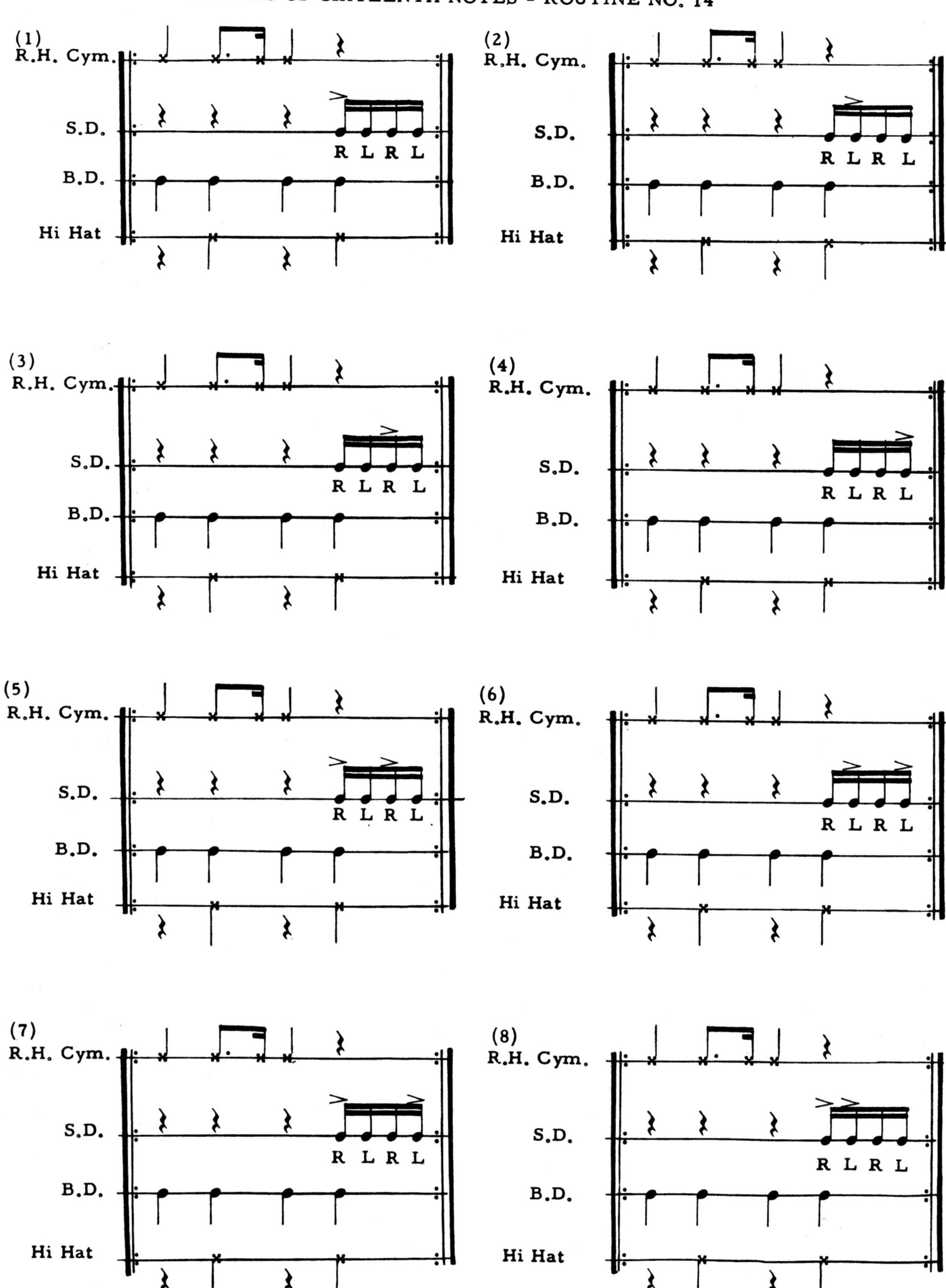

LEFT HAND INDEPENDENCE - R.H., B.D. and Hi HAT.
Play all eighth, dotted eighth and sixteenth notes as written.

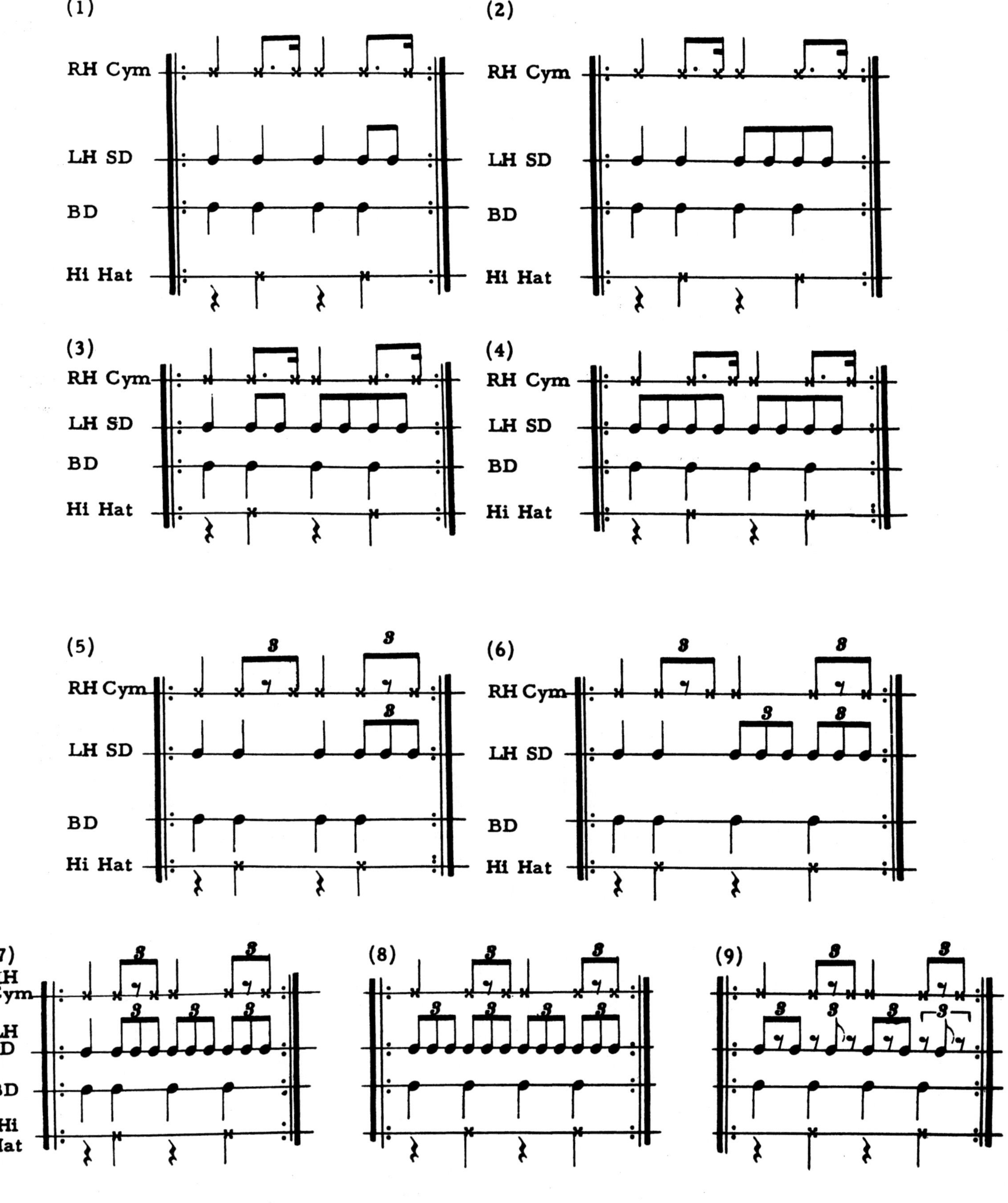

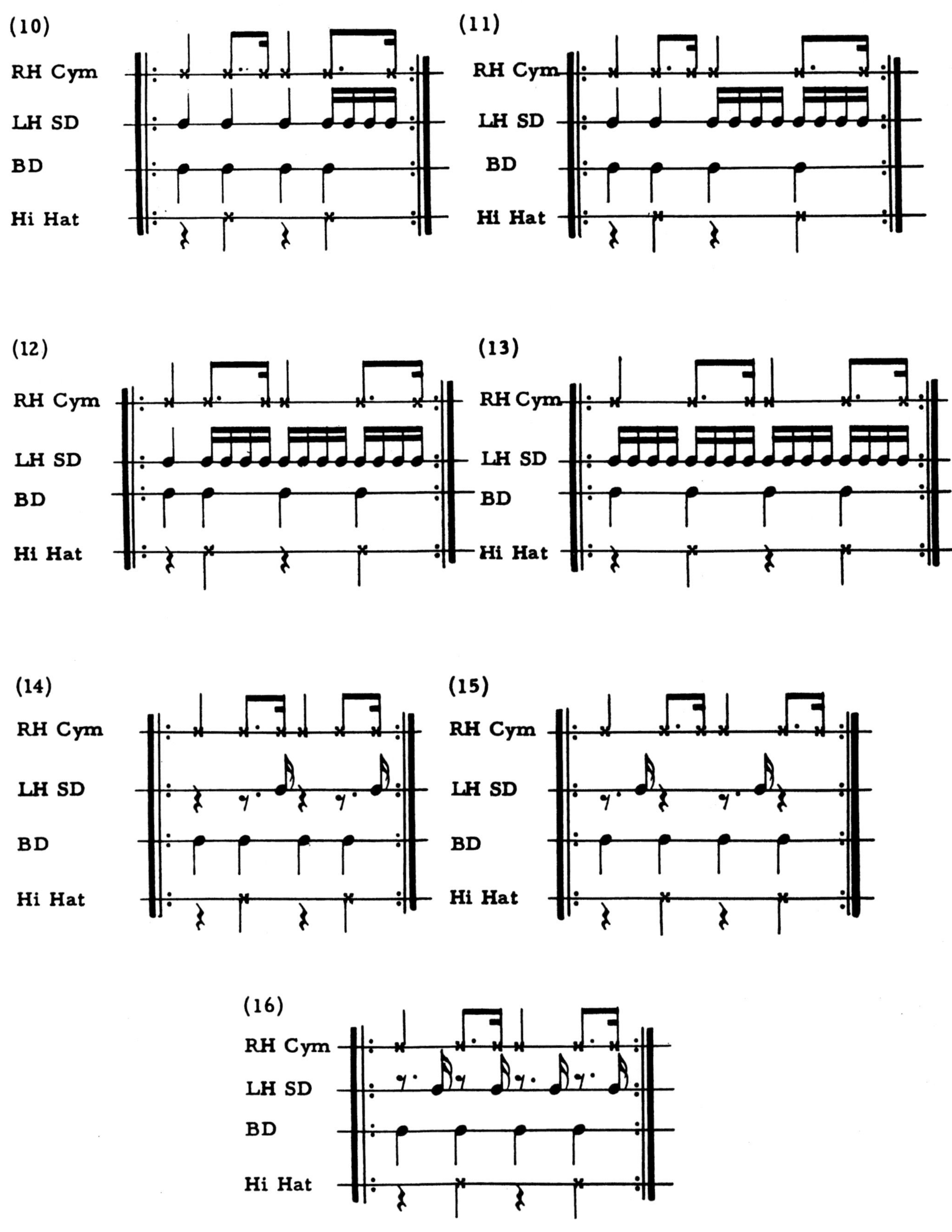
(10)
RH Cym
LH SD
BD
Hi Hat
(11)
RH Cym
LH SD
BD
Hi Hat
(12)
RH Cym
LH SD
BD
Hi Hat
(13)
RH Cym
LH SD
BD
Hi Hat
(14)
RH Cym
LH SD
BD
Hi Hat
(15)
RH Cym
LH SD
BD
Hi Hat
(16)
RH Cym
LH SD
BD
Hi Hat

BASS DRUM INDEPENDENCE - R.H., B.D. and Hi Hat

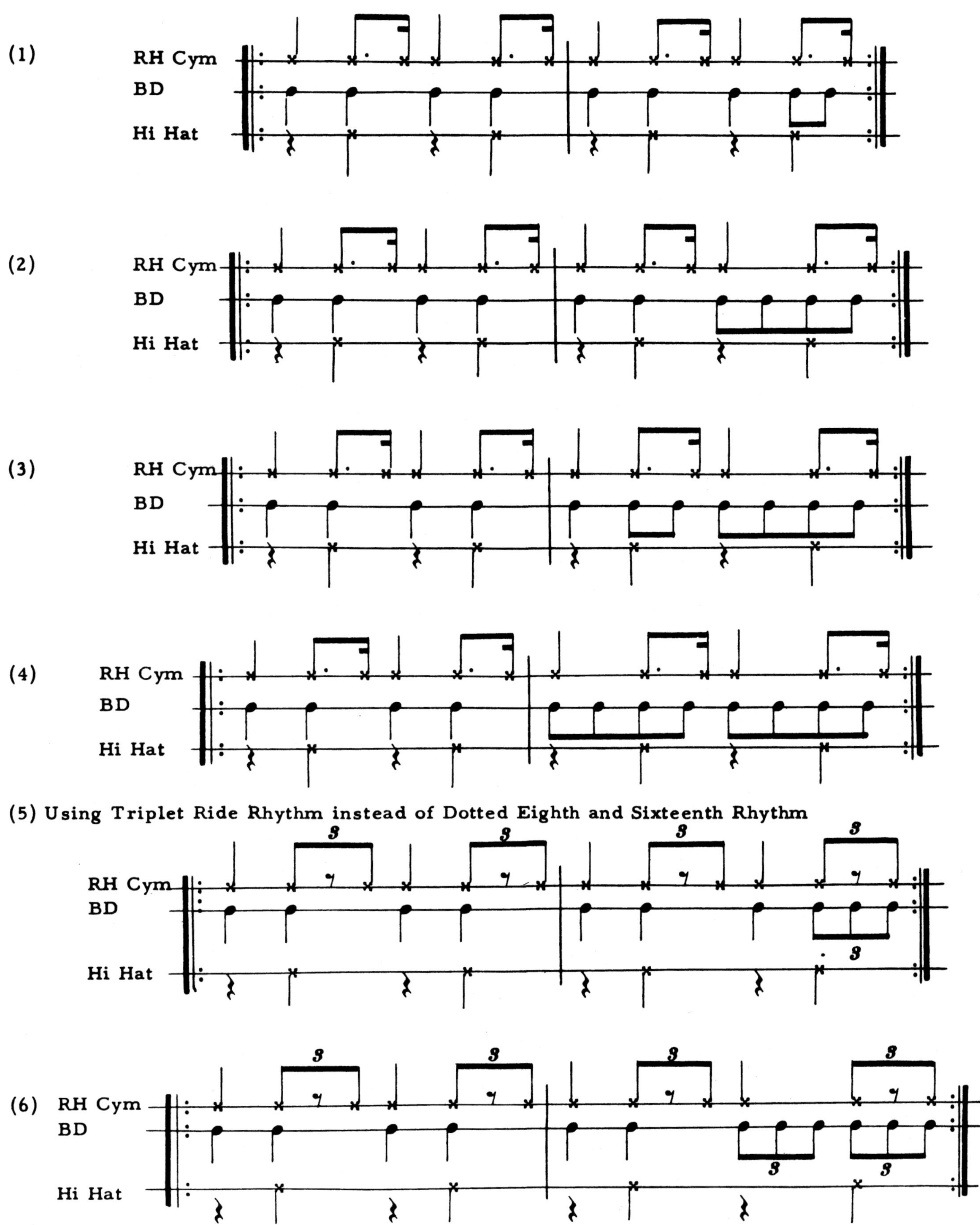

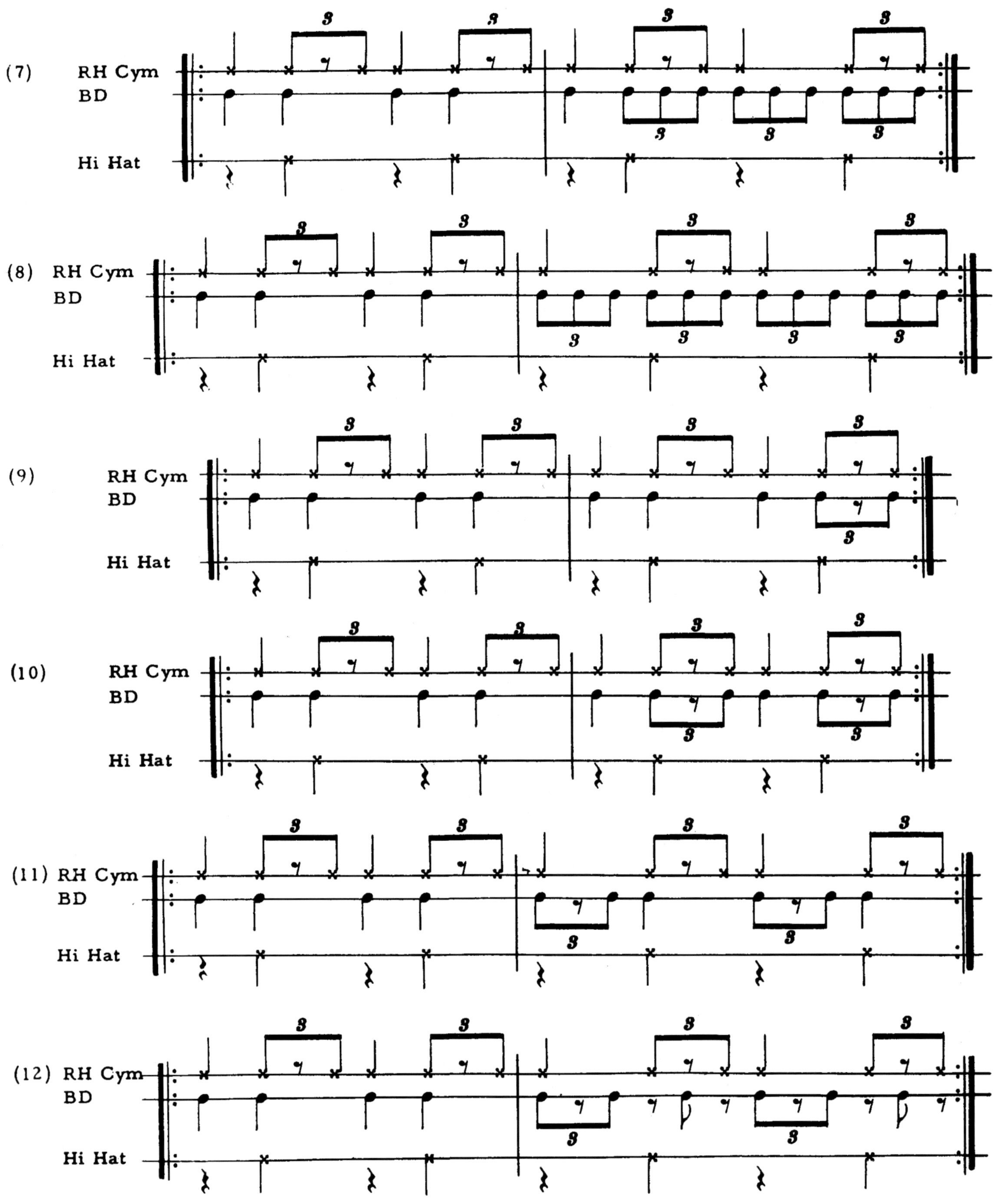
(7)
RH Cym
BD
Hi Hat
(8)
RH Cym
BD
Hi Hat
(9)
RH Cym
BD
Hi Hat
(10)
RH Cym
BD
Hi Hat
(11)
RH Cym
BD
Hi Hat
(12)
RH Cym
BD
Hi Hat

SMALL TOM-TOM, SNARE DRUM, BASS DRUM, HI HAT ROUTINES

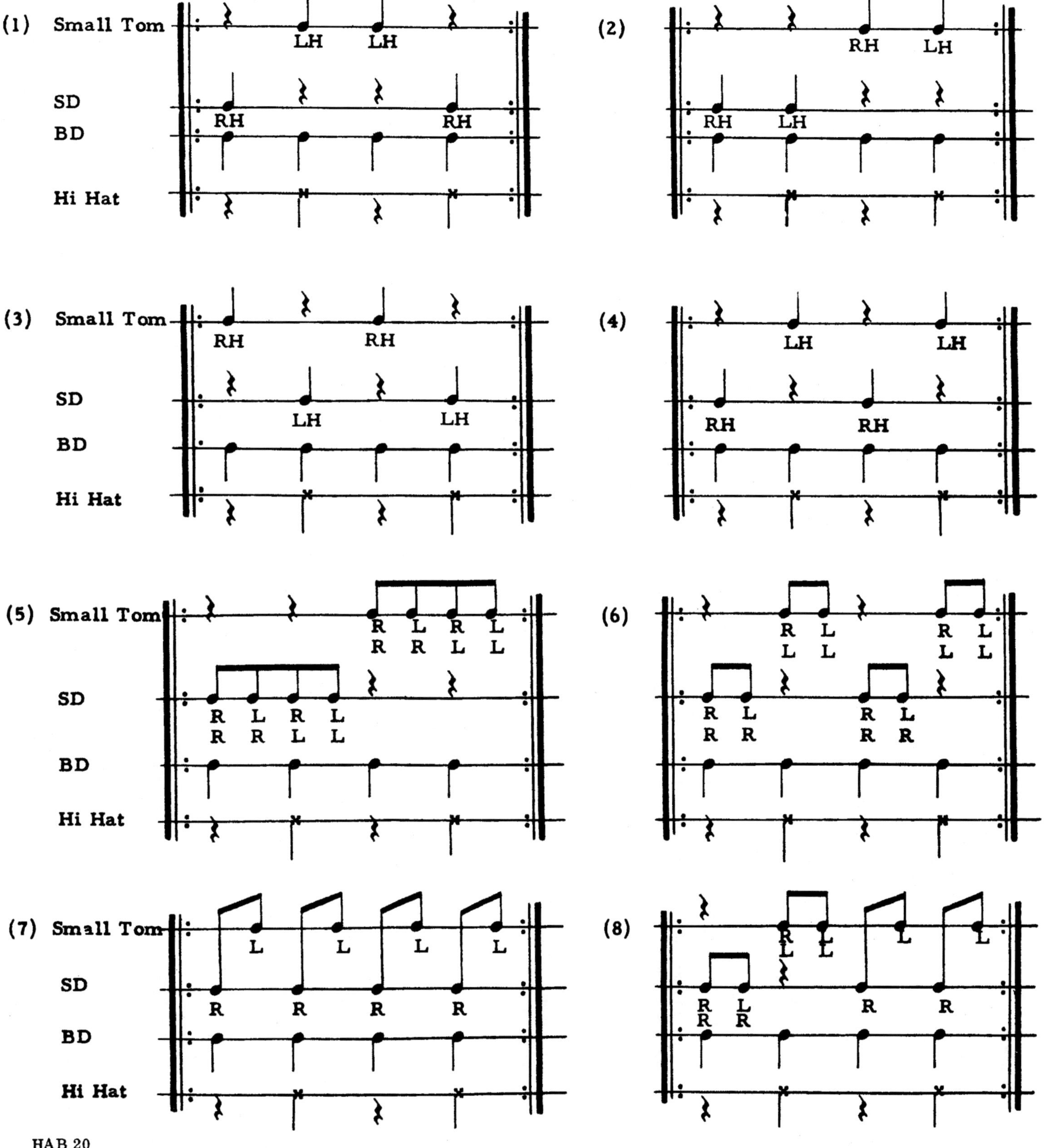

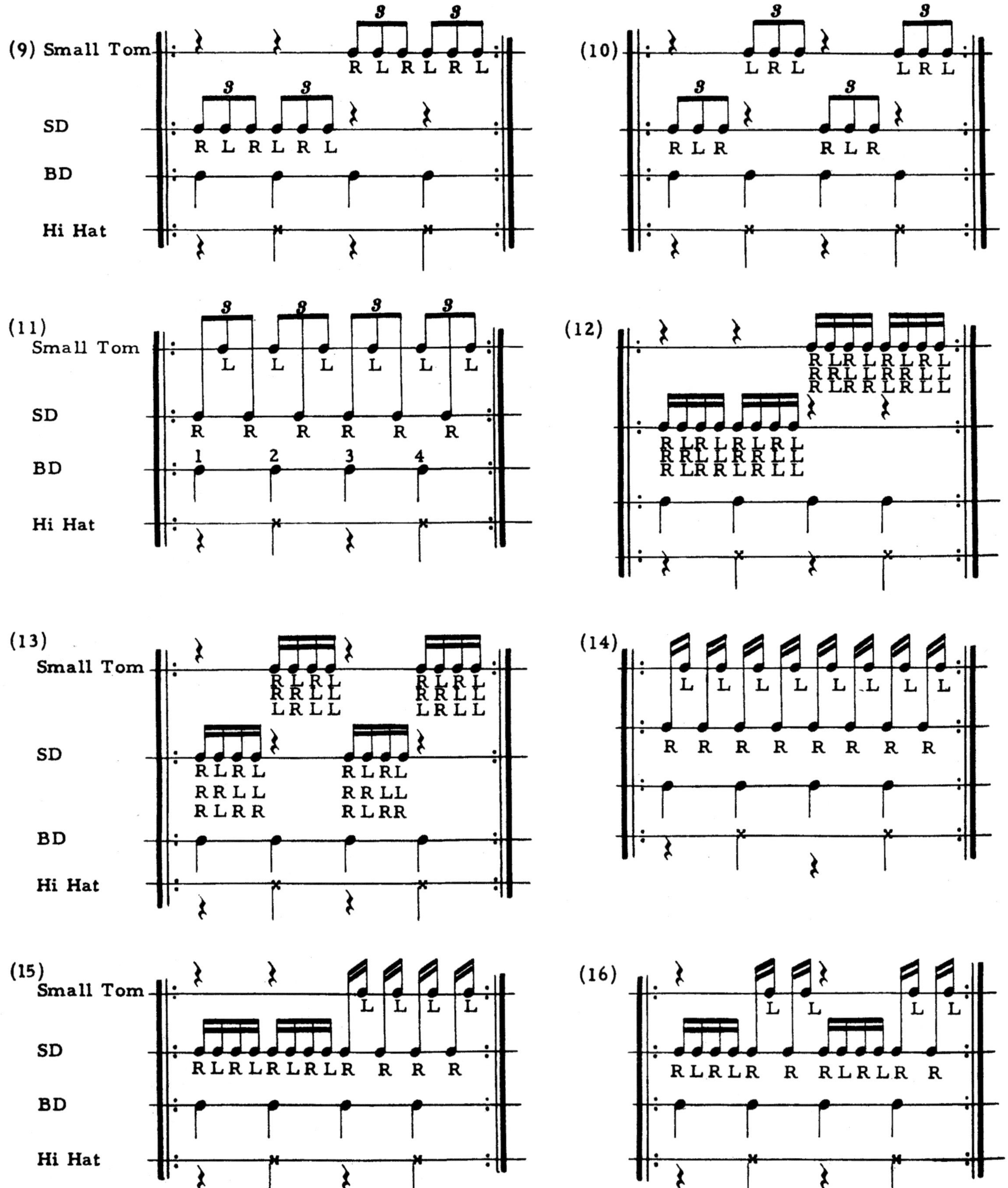
(9) Small Tom
SD
BD
Hi Hat
R L R L R L
R L R L R L
(10)
L R L
L R L
R L R
R L R
(11)
Small Tom
SD
BD
Hi Hat
L L L L L L
R R R R R R
1 2 3 4
(12)
R L R L R L R L
R R L L R R L L
R L R R L R L L
R L R L R L R L
R R L L R R L L
R L R R L R L L
(13)
Small Tom
SD
BD
Hi Hat
R L R L
R R L L
L R L L
R L R L
R R L L
L R L L
R L R L
R R L L
R L R R
R L R L
R R L L
R L R R
(14)
L L L L L L L L
R R R R R R R R
(15)
Small Tom
SD
BD
Hi Hat
L L L L
R L R L R L R L R R R R
(16)
L L L L
R L R L R R R L R L R R